Matt Taibbi and Shellenger Michael: Twitter Files Hearing Eruption

By

Gregory D. Richardson

Copyright

Table of Contents

Chapter 1: Matt Taibbi's Open Statement Before the Hearing

Before testifying before the House Judiciary Committee on Thursday on the Twitter Files, independent journalist Matt Taibbi released his opening statement. In it, he warned that the documents show a threat to Americans' First Amendment rights.

When several executives struggled to explain how it violated their "hacked materials" policy, Taibbi's first chapter of the series, which focused on Twitter's internal talks leading to it censoring the Hunter Biden laptop story during the 2020 presidential race, went viral.

The Twitter Files have also shown censoring attempts by the offices of Rep. Adam Schiff (D-Calif.), the Trump and Biden White Houses, and others. Other parts exposed Twitter's "blacklisting" of well-known conservatives, provided a behind-the-scenes look at Trump's suspension from the service, and shed light on Twitter's strong links to the FBI. A thorough investigation of Hamilton 68, a so-called "dashboard" that created the false appearance of massive Russian bot activity, has also been done by Taibbi.

"I arrived at this location today as a result of a chain of events that started late last year when I got a letter from a source online. Are you interested in looking into the censorship and manipulation that Twitter engaged in in-depth?' it asked. The first of what became known as the "Twitter Files" reports was released a week later, "Taibbi went on. "It would be an understatement to say that they drew a great deal of public attention. Only the initial tweet about the blocking of the Hunter Biden laptop story garnered 143 million impressions and 30 million interactions, making my computer seem to be a slot machine."

As other journalists, like Michael Shellenberger and Bari Weiss, joined him in revealing Twitter's once-private internal discussions, Taibbi stated that he started to "understand the magnitude of this story."

"The Internet was first expected to democratize international knowledge sharing. A free internet would defeat all efforts to regulate information flow, posing a danger to all authoritarian regimes throughout the world "Taibbi wrote. "What we discovered in the Files was a massive attempt to break that promise and utilize machine learning and other methods to censor and socially manage the internet. Sadly, it looks like our administration is taking the lead."

While highlighting interactions between government officials and Twitter executives, Taibbi gave "the first clues" of this. He informed the House Judiciary Committee that a fresh Twitter Files thread detailing how "tens of thousands of emails led to a series of disclosures" will be published.

Elon Musk, the owner of Twitter, has made a strong case for transparency about Twitter's past and current activities in terms of content curation on the network.

"We discovered that Twitter, Facebook, Google, and other businesses established a formal system for receiving "requests" for moderation from all branches of the government, including the CIA, DHS, HHS, DOD, and the Global Engagement Center at State. There were probably 20 quasi-private organizations monitoring Twitter for every government entity "Taibbi wrote. "Making lists of persons whose thoughts, beliefs, affiliations, or sympathies are considered "misinformation," "disinformation," or "misinformation" is a focus of this quickly expanding network. The latter phrase is just another way of saying "true but inconvenient."

He called the creation of such lists "a type of digital McCarthyism" and said that "law-abiding individuals and businesses whose sole offense is running afoul of a remote, faceless, unaccountable, algorithmic judge" might be negatively affected and turned away from companies like PayPal.

"This mechanism for punishment without due process is disturbing as someone who grew up a conventional ACLU liberal," Taibbi said.

According to the Substack journalist, the media ought to be the people's final line of defense, but "instead of looking into these organizations, journalists cooperated with them."

"If Twitter did not immediately delete an account, government organizations, and NGOs would contact reporters for the New York Times, Washington Post, and other publications, who would then contact Twitter to ask why no action had been done. In essence, press organizations turned into a state-sponsored thought-policing apparatus "Taibbi wrote.

According to Taibbi, one of the reasons why Americans are different from citizens of other nations is that "we don't allow anybody to tell us what to believe, particularly not the government."

The strongest protection against the Censorship-Industrial Complex, according to him, is the First Amendment and an American populace used to having the freedom of speech. We risk losing this most important right, without which all other democratic rights are unattainable, according to what the Twitter Files have shown.

Chapter 2: The Heated Exchange Between Matt Taibi and House Democrat

Rep. Sylvia Garcia questioned journalist Matt Taibbi repeatedly about who contacted him before the creation of the Twitter Files.

At a tense House Judiciary Committee hearing on the "Twitter Files" on Thursday, Rep. Sylvia R. Garcia, D-Texas, was accused of pressuring writer Matt Taibbi into disclosing a source, but the reporter resisted.

That was previously brought up during the hearing when Taibbi was explicitly questioned about them concerning his reporting on internal Twitter discussions and claims of government censorship, thus sourcing was a touchy issue. When Elon Musk, the owner of Twitter, initially contacted Taibbi about joining the Twitter Files initiative, which has made previously-secret internal communications public and uncovered a variety of problems, Garcia questioned Taibbi.

As Garcia argued that she only needed a date, Taibbi started to explain he couldn't provide such information.

"Unfortunately, I can't provide it to you because it involves a source, and I'm a journalist. I keep my sources private, "said Taibbi.

He disagreed with Garcia's assertion that chronology is more important than the source.

Taibbi said, "No, that's an issue of sources.

The Texas Democrat persisted in raising the subject.

Garcia added, "You previously said that someone had sent you a message through the internet asking whether you would be interested in receiving certain information.

Taibbi said, "Yeah, and I referred to that guy as a source.

So you won't tell us when Musk initially contacted you, Garcia questioned.

Once again, Congresswoman, you're requiring a reporter to disclose a source, Taibbi said.

Taibbi was unamused when Garcia questioned if he thought Musk was the direct source.

I am unable to respond to your question because you are now attempting to convince me that he is the source, Taibbi responded.

Garcia said that Musk is a source and that this is the "only logical conclusion," but Taibbi informed her she was "free to infer" anything she wanted.

Rep. Jim Jordan, R-Ohio, head of the House Judiciary Committee, stepped in and Garcia said, "You can't have it both ways.

Jordan answered, "He can, he's a journalist," igniting a fight among the group.

Ranking Member Stacey Plaskett, D-Virgin Islands, who had a similar conversation with Taibbi previously, said that since Taibbi wouldn't comment on Musk, it must indicate the Twitter owner was the source of the issue. Many members shouted over each other aggressively.

Jordan reacted angrily, "He's not going to identify his source and the fact that Democrats are forcing him to do so is such a violation of the First Amendment.

Plaskett earlier in the hearing questioned Taibbi who provided him access to the emails that were made public in the Twitter Files, but Taibbi refused to tell.

"Sources at Twitter are credited for my article," he claimed.

Jordan then questioned Plaskett about whether or whether she was attempting to get reporters to divulge their sources, but she refuted the charge

Chapter 3 : Representative Stacey Plaskett Accuses the "Twitter Files" Reporters

During a hearing on the Twitter Files on Thursday, Representative Stacey Plaskett (D-Virgin Islands) lashed out at Matt Taibbi and Michael Shellenberger, claiming that their reporting on how the social media platform collaborated with various federal agencies to censor unpopular political viewpoints put the lives of Twitter employees in danger.

During the first round of questioning, Plaskett, the ranking member of the Select Committee on the Weaponization of the Federal Government, used her allotted time to dismiss the witnesses' worries that the FBI and other federal agencies might pressure Twitter to take action against users who disseminate alleged "disinformation" on a range of politically charged topics. Instead of criticizing the government's censorship of political expression, Plaskett chastised the witnesses for supposedly putting Twitter workers at risk by releasing their redacted internal messages.

"Mr. Chairman, I'm not exaggerating when I say that you have two witnesses in front of you who directly threaten anyone who disagrees with them. When individuals experience it, isn't it amusing? At the laughing of committee chairman Jim Jordan, Plaskett said, "This is intolerable.

Plaskett maintained that there was no "real proof" of collaboration between Twitter and the federal government and said that the many emails made public by Shellenberger and Taibbi only serve as a byproduct of lawful "content moderation" operations.

Plaskett continued by citing the testimony of Yoel Roth, a former director of trust and safety at Twitter, who claimed in a previous committee hearing that he had experienced threats and online harassment after his involvement in content censorship at the FBI's request was revealed by the Twitter Files reporting.

The Democratic representative from Florida, Debbie Wasserman Schultz, used a similar line of inquiry, saying, "Being a Republican witness today surely throws a shadow over your neutrality."

As "Elon Musk's preferred journalist," Schultz continued to disparage Taibbi.

"Elon Musk spoon-fed you his carefully chosen facts, which you must have known would at the very least give rise to a right-wing conspiracy theory or at the very least, would encourage a biased perspective. The Florida delegate pointed a finger at Taibbi and said, "You broke your own rule and you seem to have benefited from it.

Later on in the hearing, Taibbi made it clear that he was given unrestricted access to internal Twitter discussions and that he had discovered censorship initiatives aimed both against right- and left-wing media outlets, users, and groups.

Since the publication of the first volume of the Twitter Files in December 2022, investigative journalists have made it known that the social media behemoth actively collaborated with federal law enforcement organizations and developed "secret blacklists" that were intended to target prominent conservative commentators.

www.ingramcontent.com/pod-product-compliance
Lightning Source LLC
Chambersburg PA
CBHW071031260726
48662CB00024B/2312